LOVE FOR CROATIA
Journeys to the Front Line
1991 - 2008
by
Hazel Hendry

Hazel Hendry with Paddy Ashdown

LOVE FOR CROATIA:

Journeys to the Front Line 1991 - 2008

First Published in 2020 by FastPrint Publishing

Peterborough, England.

A CIP catalogue record for this book is available from the British Library

Paperback ISBN 9781784567392

Printed and bound in England by

www.printondemand-worldwide.com

www.fast-print.net/bookshop

INDEX

INTRODUCTION   1
HOW IT ALL BEGAN   7
NOTES FROM SOME OF MY EARLIEST VISITS   9
WAR AND ITS HORRORS   13
A CUSTOMS OFFICIAL   16
SLAVEN AND IGOR   19
OSIJEK 1992   21
VINKOVCI – ŽUPANJA – LIPIK 1992   23
NUŠTAR Early 1992 -1993   27
PAKRAC AND LIPIK – GHOST TOWNS Early 1993   30
DUHOVNA STVARNOST 1995   34
ZORAN FILIPOVIĆ 1991   37
ŽUPANJA – JACOVAR – SLAVONSKI BROD 1992   39
LASLOVO 1994   44
OTHER VISITS TO ŽUPANJA – VINKOVCI 1993 - 1994   46
OSIJEK (MY MAIN TOWN) 1994   49
HELP FOR OSIJEK PRISON 1993   52
OSIJEK PRISON AND CHILDREN'S HOMES 1995   55
AT LAST, SOME PRISONERS HOME 1993   59
MASS GRAVES 1991 -? (still being found in 2012)   62
FIGHTING IN THE STREET 1994   65
DARKO, FRANO AND MARIJA 1992   69
THE MATUSINOVIĆ FAMILY   77
THE JELENIĆ FAMILY   80
THANK YOU   81
DONATIONS FOR HOSPITALS 1998   83
MATTHEW BIGWOOD 1996   86
THE NUNNERY Summer 1997   89
A NEWSLETTER   91
ANOTHER NEWSLETTER   94
PRESENTATION of PAUL HARRIS AWARD from ROTARY CLUB OF STROUD   96
SOME THOUGHTS BEFORE NEXT VISIT November-December 1996   98
CHRISTMAS AND OTHER GIFTS 1997   99
AND FINALLY 2012   102
ACKNOWLEDGEMENTS   104
CONCLUSION   106
THE FRONT LINE AROUND OSIJEK, DAKOVO, VINKOVCI and VUKOVAR   112

INTRODUCTION

Hazel Hendry in her own words
based on a piece written in 1997

My name is Hazel Hendry and, at the time of my Journals, I lived in the Cotswolds with my lovely children Julie and Adam. Julie was a nurse and Adam was studying Social Work at Bath University.

I am an extremely proud Mum and love them both immensely. As for me, I have been a secretary, a nurse and voluntary worker helping people in many ways. I walked from John O'Groats to Lands End and from Ramsgate to Fishguard in Wales. (From the north to the south of the UK and the east to the west, you will see I walked the sign of The Cross). Money raised from these walks went to help TEARFUND. I have been a Christian for many, many years.

I always knew there would be work for me to do for the Lord and this came unexpectedly from a 'phone call I had from Rev George Hoffman whilst he was in Croatia. He said, 'The people in Croatia need your help'. After the call, I sat and said to Our Lord, 'OK Father, I will do this work but You must give me all that I will need.' HE did in abundance, greatly.

Hazel in the cab of an aid lorry

Now for over six years, I have arranged and organised 39 vehicles holding 39 tons each of much needed aid in the way of clothes, shoes, bed linen, towels, small furniture, carpets, glassware, crockery, cutlery, toys, games, bicycles, pianos, tables, chairs, three piece suites, spades, forks, brushes, cookers, washing machines, dish washers, the lists are endless. Whatever has been requested, mainly from the town of Osijek, I have tried to collect in the United Kingdom and deliver to them.

The hospitals in this region have long lists of requests, and a massive quantity was delivered to Osijek Hospitals, including defibrillators, anaesthetic machines, wheel chairs, operating tables, dressings, swabs, needles sutures, bed linen, toiletries, baby food, glassware, crockery, X-ray films and plates, ECG Electrodes, Urological Equipment, the list goes on and on..... I tried to give whatever was requested.

Beneficiaries of this aid have been Children's Homes, Schools, Ivan Filipović received the beautiful electric organ, which I know will give much pleasure to many children in Osijek for many years to come, Osijek Prison, Orphanages,

Refugee Camps, Hospitals, and many, many individuals. It has been a personal joy since 1992 to give gifts to the children of Osijek for St Nicholas.

You will read that dates and times in my Journals were insignificant. This happens because so many villages, hospitals, children's homes, and many, many places needed to be visited. There is so much to do, so many in need, their need for help is desperate, their lives have been destroyed. So, once I had been to Zagreb the desire inside me was to get to the Front Line; even into the very Front Line. My heart goes out to Croatia, their suffering is immense.

I have many special friends in Croatia. One, more than anyone else I place in very high esteem, his name is Darko Skugor, my translator. He travels with me wherever I have needed to go, a gentleman who put himself between me and the Chetniks when we delivered aid to Slavonski Brod and were down by the river. He did this on many, many, occasions and I was always aware of what he was doing. He was always with me during the 'bad' times, always kind, helpful and understanding in what I have tried to do. His wife Drenka is also a friend of mine and I dearly love their son, Filip.

Then there is Frano and Marija Matusnovic, their daughter Kristina, Professor Dr Srećko Jelenić and his lovely wife Zvonka. Dr Mladen Pajtler and Dr Dalibor Koprolćec from the hospital. All members of the staff in Osijek Prison,

4

Custom Officials, I could go on, but I will just end with a lady who has shown extreme kindness to me, Jadranka Filipović, in whose home I mainly stay. I thank her for this.

I thank everyone in the United Kingdom for their extreme generosity, caring and kindness in making all this possible, the Hospitals, the Companies, Newspapers and local Radio Stations, and of course, men and women just like me who really care.

The Croatian Embassy in Conway Street in London helped me tremendously by giving me details of towns and villages which were in dire need of help and it was through talking with Dr Drago Stambuk (he was Charge d'Affaires) that I really realised that I needed to get to the very front-line. Dr Stambuk was extremely helpful and interested in this work which was happening for his country. Dr Stambuk went on to be Ambassador for Croatia in India.

The person who helped me most of all, however, was Andrija Kojakovic who went on to be Ambassador for Croatia in September 1997 – October 2002. He was always available when I needed advice and when he came back to the UK from Croatia and I was about to leave to go there, at Heathrow (this happened many times our visits crossed) Andrija always spoke to me to ask where I was off to, was I alright, and he was always interested in knowing what was being taken over to help those in need back in his home of Croatia, and, when would I get back home.

First Secretary of the Croatian Embassy, Jasmin Devlic, Hazel Hendry and Croatian Amassador Andrija Kojakovic

I liked Andrija and it was a joy to eventually meet his family, his lovely wife, Stela, and his two beautiful daughters. Once they visited my home in Gloucestershire and the girls went horse riding in the countryside with my daughter Julie. A lovely time far away from war, and a time to remember.

I organised dinners in Painswick Hotel for anyone who had helped the folk of Croatia in any way. There was never an empty seat and all had paid for their own meal, such lovely evenings to remember. Dr Stambuk attended one with Andrija and Stela who attended many.

I thank God for this work He has given me to do. And I ask that God will continue to bring **PEACE** in Croatia, and may God Bless the brave little town on Osijek, which was almost brought down on its knees in a vicious and violent war……… Almost, but not quite.

Long Live Croatia

Hazel Hendry
22nd October 1997

Note: the passage in italics was added prior to this publication.

HOW IT ALL BEGAN 1991 - 1992

It all began in November 1991. The Chetniks (Serbian Army) attacked and killed Croatian guards on sentry duty on the border of Croatia and Serbia.

Croatia was not prepared or ready for war so the first attack on Vukovar was frightening, utterly evil and utterly devastating as this lovely town was systematically blown to pieces and its inhabitants killed.

My work began in Zagreb visiting centres, hospitals, children's homes and meeting who and whoever I could. But I knew my work had to be on the very front-line so that is how I went to Osijek.

I did not know Croatia in peacetime, only as a war zone. Zagreb was attacked by Serbian Forces but it was nothing like what was happening further north. The areas I worked in were in Slavonija (not to be confused with Slovenia).

Travelling from Zagreb to Osijek by train we would travel though miles and miles of fields used for growing tobacco. Rich, fertile land I thought wasted. This is what Serbia wanted: Croatia and its land. This was a 'territorial' war, not as many thought a 'religious' war.

There were to be eventually over one thousand mass graves, total destruction everywhere, men and boys (as young as 15) rounded up, believed to have dug their own graves then shot in the back of their heads. The more mass graves I saw the more I turned to Our Dear Lord and Father. I have never understood why He gave me this work to do, but I always did my best. Jesus never said He would stop these things from happening but He did say He would help us through them, and he certainly helped me.

NOTES FROM SOME OF MY EARLIEST VISITS

Families give refreshments to Hazel on Arrival

The shock to see so many refugees and hear at first hand of the way people were forced to leave their homes really shook me. The sheer terror and horror what they felt through my empathy I could feel too. I didn't think such atrocities were possible.

Within minutes of arriving at Duhovna Stvarnost in Zagreb, news came that 200 women with small children were about to arrive. What I saw and heard from these ladies was just too much to bear as they told me about being 'rounded up' in their village by Serbs and their men and boys were tortured and then shot in front of them. Tears fell down my face and mingled with theirs as I hugged people around me to show the compassion I was feeling. These poor people, no clothes, no food, no husbands and their older sons killed. There were no homes to return to for they were forced to watch as each individual home was systematically destroyed. Where would they go, how would they even survive, where could they live?

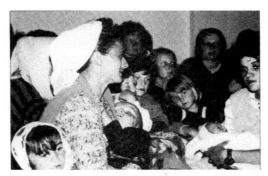

Children Stare Wide-eyed

Duhovna Stvarnost would look after them. They would provide food, clothes and accommodation for these people, even move them to safer areas away from the war zone. No one can turn back the clock, no one remove what has happened, but God promised to help everyone through storms and He is much stronger than any evil power that is at work in this country of Croatia and its neighbour Bosnia. He will not desert these people in their hour of need.

It was here in Zagreb I met a woman who had been raped. I was told over and again about deplorable conditions of detention centres for women and girls. How guards beat these women and girls into submission for their sexual game. How they made these poor females strip and then be passed from one man to another. I was told of one girl being made to dance near a broken and shelled church; she was also made to sing lewd and filthy songs. Then in front of her family she was raped. I was told her age was just 11 years. This girl's story is only one of so many I heard. It seems men in the Serbian and Chetnik armies are surrounded by wicked and evil forces for these terrible acts which are controlling them are so barbaric and sub-human.

Another visit took me to the Mosque in Zagreb. Surrounding it were 700-800 Moslems waiting for food and water. They had nowhere to go only the Mosque to turn to, for these poor and wretched people had no money, no papers, no food or clothes. They couldn't go forward and they certainly couldn't go back.

Inside the Mosque there was a deep and dreadful shock for there must have been nearly 3,000 people milling around. Families huddled together, children crying, men, women and children with looks of sheer desperation in their tired and drained faces which were also filled with fear. There was hardly room to move around. Eventually, a group of us were taken into a small room. We removed our shoes and were greeted by Irfan Ivanovic (he was the ex-Vice President of Yugoslavia). This man spoke of the evils of war, he told of 600 churches, 700 hospitals and a million homes had been destroyed. Gone too was 75% of machinery, all Croatians together with vineyards, all destroyed. 5,000 pigs had been slaughtered; even Lippizzan horses cruelly killed by each one having one leg chopped off. There were a million refugees. We were told of men simply disappearing, taken into concentration camps. Some who successfully escaped told of acts of extreme cruelty with continual beatings. Men chosen at random were shot, others always treated with brutality and even more beatings. There was no food or drink. It is no wonder pictures later appearing on TV of starving skeletal men as these camps went on to be discovered. These pictures went on to shock the whole world about what was going on.

The distribution centre in central Zagreb, now nearly a year later, is going well, but I feel the need to move further away from Zagreb to help people who have not so far been reached. But, what happens here in Zagreb, when people (refugees) reach here, they then register with the centre and get the help they may, and do, need. Under these terrible circumstances I look at these people with great respect and admiration. They look clean and tidy, their children, though tense and strained are usually very well behaved. The children seem to understand that everyone is watching out and over them. People at home sometimes say to me 'Oh, those poor children' but I remind them that children run or be carried. It is the poor old people that are left behind that should have the pity, for their survival is bleak.

WAR AND ITS HORRORS

During the Spring of 1992, I visited Osijek, a front line surrounded on three sides by the attacking Serbs was a heart breaking one. People everywhere, my friends, doctors, pharmacists, prison officials, simply everyone just waiting for the wailing sound of the 'general alert' to start ringing out once again.

In Sarvas, three refuse collectors and their vehicle were taken by Chetniks, officially called Serbs. Four young soldiers were sent to be investigated ending up losing their legs after being blown up by mines left behind by these Serbs. I had met the doctor sent to the shocking and devastating scene. He was sickened by these scenes.

Most nights were disturbed by continual shooting, tanks moving around on the other side of the River Drava and then later hearing about individuals being shot in different villages around Osijek. One evening whilst sitting talking, a round of machine gun fire went past the window of the flat I was in. Children had been playing there only an hour before. I was told this was intended for me as a warning to 'keep away'. But I couldn't. Among other brief notes I have found in my folders is this one:

Explosion, very loud, a mine? 6.45 am 3rd July, again in the evening. 10th July machine gun fire outside here yet again – disconcerting!! Gun shots again 11th July. Feel so sorry for the people of Osijek, heavy shooting again during the

14

night 12th July from over the Drava. Explosions seem nearer – and so it all goes on. Other places I visit are Županja, Rasino Selo and Ridjana Posavski. These have been badly bombarded too during the last two weeks. (These places are being attacked from Brcko which is north of Tuzla. My heart cries out to these people in Croatia and Bosnia for they are suffering so deeply and tragically. Here in the peacefulness of our country it is hard to imagine the horrors of this war in The Balkans, but it really is out there. I have shared this for the last four years with so many and it is only with Our Lord's help and support with prayer and all the help given I can carry on this work. I have been with

War damaged buildings in Nuštar

so many helpless, suffering people in Vukovar, Pakrac, Lipik, Slavonski Brod, Nuštar, Osijek, Vinkovci to name a few places, the horrors of war evil and shocking.

I have seen and been with all the horrors of this war so much so I can never tell it all. The cruel and barbaric minds are hard to understand but one thing drives me on, the Lord gave me a job to do and I will do my best to see it through. It is God, my love and trust in Him and my complete faith in this work he has given me to do is what sees me through all of this war. I do not doubt when I look back over the years of work I did as a Christian, I was in fact being trained for this work I am doing now in these frontline towns. I say this because there is absolutely no way could I do what I do without some training or without God. I get on with my work and am totally supported by people home in England and everyone in the Slavonija region of Croatia.

I intend to return in September and December. I appealed for blankets, sheets, pillows and cases, towels, clothes (men's especially), shoes, food, medical items and toiletries and of course I always need money for lorries, £1,250 each visit. The situation is urgent as there is a general alert in Osijek. God help them.

Eventually, the cost rose to £2,500 per lorry and finally, 49 lorries were sent to Croatia, all filled with medical aid, food, toiletries, blankets – all bed linen, curtains, artificial limbs, a dentist chair, operating table and even furniture. (Most of the furniture went to Laslovo). People in the UK never stopped giving, even people in France, Spain and USA sent items.

A CUSTOMS OFFICIAL

These notes would be of an early delivery as that was the only time I travelled through France etc.

The lorry travelled through France, Germany, Hungary and into Croatia with no problems at all. The important paperwork was correct – thanks to Darko Skugor – as this all helped the driver to get through these borders promptly and quickly. Strangely, it was a different story when reaching Croatia. The Customs official was excitable and saying everything should be brought in through the Red Cross or Caritas or some other large Charitable Organisation. And, it was at this stage I met up with the driver, the lorry and the humanitarian aid. (I flew in from London to Zagreb £99.00 return), and it was while I listened to this small loud man I realized how quickly people forget, how quickly it is forgotten that it is people like me who came to Croatia when the war there started, who have never ceased to take aid to the front line, who never ceased to care about the refugees, Churches, Homes, Hospitals and just everyone in this beautiful but now devastated country. And it seems the 'little people' like me can now be forgotten. I find this distressing and it makes me feel sad and I find it unbearable that a little man in Customs (Croatia) can make things so difficult.

For example, when I was here in December 1993, I was asked if I could help people in Slavonski Brod by giving them as much help as I could, and the same request for the prison in Osijek. So, appealing to many Churches and individuals as was possible at home, a tremendous amount of aid was collected for these places, as had been for Vinkovci and Osijek hospitals many times before. There were large quantities of mixed medicines and various tablets and drugs all donated by Doctors and people back home. But, so much fuss was made about the things for Slavonski Brod and the prison that was quite incredible. In the end the prison could only receive these things if they went through official channels. I should add this response was the same for the home for children by the pharmacy in Osijek, who have in fact, received items from me each time I visit Osijek. Disappointing, to say the least.

It also now seems that all medicines, etc, I bring I must be present when these are given out. What on earth is happening!!! I appeal in big ways in England to get help for those suffering in Croatia and I find this 'officialdom' is tiresome and unnecessary. Why can't people just accept that people care enough to bring aid to their country especially those like me who have travelled and worked extremely hard, I should add, to help these devastated people. I understand that officials should know of all aid taken into a country, I understand this totally, but these rude officials should also know that I came to help them when no one else did. The saddest thing of all that it was a little, round man in the Customs office in Osijek who brought these things to mind. Especially sad, that this happened in Osijek as this was in the area I have cared for people the most, whose suffering is shocking, too many killed and lots more injured. Dreadful.

PS. I should mention here this was the only time there was difficulty with an official. After this time, the lorries sent with aid via me to Croatia sailed through Customs.

It sounds as this is read that it is all about me. Not true, I was just very upset by this really very rude man, and I would never forget why I was doing HIS work for that was so much more important and very urgently needed. When Our Lord's work is needed to be done, sometimes a little devil tries to hamper His work, and mine!

SLAVEN AND IGOR

During a very hot early summer of 1994, I was asked by Srećko Jelenić if I would call to see Slaven, the young lad who tried to hang himself when Osijek was under attack. His grandma found him and cut what he had put around his neck. Slaven is now in a vegetative state and will never recover, but, his mum and dad need help and that is where I can be of use, thanks to all those people back home. I was

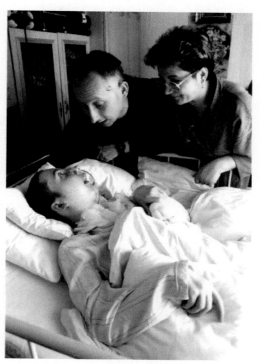

Slaven

able to give them food, toiletries and money. It all helps them. Dear Lord, please take great care of Slaven and Igor, they need your love and comfort. I never forget why I am here but everyone knows I am doing the Lord's work. This war has been such a shocking, atrocious and awful war with neighbour killing neighbour simply because they are not Serbian. Many Serbs I have met have changed their names to a Croatian one now; that helps only a few, though.

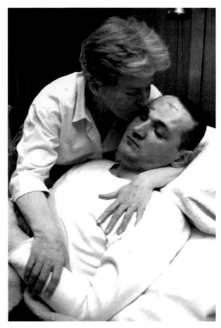

Igor

Once again, in the summer of late 1994, when visiting Igor on an extremely hot day, I found his room full of people. His mother (meaning well) was constantly stroking Igor's head and I knew immediately that wasn't good for Igor as shrapnel was still lodged in his head. I asked if I could sit by Igor, poor man. He was so very hot. I asked for a cloth warmed with water, then gently wiped Igor's face. His mother jumped up extremely worried and said, "Don't do that he will get cold" (so translated by Darko!). So, of course, I stopped but I still feel that was better for Igor. I spent a lot of time praying for these families and always asked people back in the UK to pray for them too. There were many serious injuries in this war but I was told what had happened to Igor was one of the worst. He was a soldier clearing land mines. He trod on a booby trap and was extremely and seriously injured.

Igor eventually died with pneumonia and Slaven stayed in his vegetative state for a long time before he died too. I helped these families as much as I could for there was no financial help for them from any organisation.

OSIJEK 1992

The devastation done by the shelling and bombing, firing of guns and previous grenades which were thrown to anything which moved had been going on for eight months. The solid fighting has certainly left its marks in a horrific and terrifying way with massive holes on roofs of nearly all houses and buildings pockmarked where bullets were aimed directly at them. How these people in Osijek kept their sanity I do not know but I certainly felt the pain which they had suffered and are suffering.

Osijek is on the border of the warring factions and because of this I find the hospitality and kindness shown to me is simply incredible. Everywhere I go, people offer me food and drink; it seems everyone wants, and needs, to give me something. It is utterly and totally moving. I shall never forget this place.

It was here I met Frano Matusinović and his wife Marija, and I was also to meet here the one person who was always to be by my side, Darko Skugor, his wife was named Drenka and their baby son Filip.

Darko was the most important person to me for he translated everything from one to another. Once we were at lunch with a priest, there were six guests. People talked a lot, when I looked around there were five empty plates and one full one. It was Darko's, for he had been translating! He and I found this amusing! Strangely, Darko made me laugh in some very tight corners we found ourselves in. Can you imagine driving in the darkness of night, no lights allowed, well, we did many times, my head would hang out of one window and Darko's the other, steering at the same time. Yes, Darko was, and is still, a very great friend. He was a great Blessing from Our Lord, and I thanked Him.

It was in Osijek I stayed most of the time. It was kind people who found a bed for me like Jadranka Filipović and then later, Professor and Dr Strecko Jelenić. I was Strecko who asked me to write my details in his address book. When I opened it I looked at Strecko and said, "I can't write here". He looked at me and said, "why not?" It was only after I mentioned that my name was to go under the 'Prince of Habsburg' he understood. Even so, I wrote in my details. It was just one of those things that make you smile.

VINKOVCI – ŽUPANJA – LIPIK 1992

Today, Sunday, we are going into dangerous territory and we are being led by a car in front by someone who takes us there with care. We are swooping around about 80 miles out of our way to get to Vinkovci and Županja. There was fighting here last night at around midnight and so we shall be there to witness the devastation of the horrors which happened. Danger yes, but I felt no fears. I just believed and trusted that God was holding me safely in His hands.

Vinkovci Hospital

Vinkovci: What a shock, the whole hospital practically blown to smithereens but still work is going on. Windows are out, whole wards not in use, no drips, no beds, no medicines, no sheets, all surgery being done underground. Heavy shooting could be heard nearby. People look so

24

desperate.   Never have I experienced such dreadful happenings. Even the men being released from the Serbian prisons couldn't upset me like this. So heart breaking.

Dr Josip Dolanski

Dr Dolanski, a very brave man, was the surgeon who stayed on in this hospital when the attacks to Vukovar, Nuštar and Vinkovci began. This is the very front line and always on a 'Red Alert'. Patients in this hospital were all killed and their bodies found in two mass graves with evidence of their having suffered physical violence before being killed. I was taken to see these graves which were in extremely lonely places and in dense wooded area. I found this heart wrenching, too much to bear.

How can man do this to his fellow brother, how could man slaughter his neighbour just because he was Croatian. I will never understand this shocking cruelty, never. My admiration for Dr Josip Dolanski was immense for he never asked who he was to operate on. Croatian or Serbian, he just did it. Dr Dolanski was an orthopaedic surgeon. Once, when I visited the hospital, Dr Dolanski, who was operating, heard I was there. I couldn't believe it when I saw this man rushing towards me. I said, "Why are you here. I thought you were operating". He looked at me and said, "I heard you were here so I told my colleagues I have to see this woman"! I made sure he went back quickly to his work but I knew by what he did that he appreciated all that was being done to help his hospital.

On another visit, we travelled to Vinkovci, the hospital always on my mind, really down on its knees but fighting to get up again. There was a reception here today as a ward for men's surgical had been reopened. It was a great joy to see this. At the reception, I gave the Senior Surgeon (Dr Dolanski) the cheque for £2000. He was clearly delighted and it will be used according to my wishes. He too gave me a certificate, and 4 bottles of wine. It is strange to receive gifts from these lovely people, they are so proud, it is hard for them to receive. This country has so little money now because of the refugees and the war but still they want to be so generous to someone like me. I really appreciate their kindness, how could I not.

There have been many explosions and firing can be heard heard spasmodically in the distance. Although when we went visiting friends of Marija and Frano last evening in Tenja the firing was simply across the road for these people live on the first front line. Here is the army of Croatian soldiers protecting the Croatian country with Serbian forces not far from the other side of them. These Serbs are a threat to Osijek, already they have taken half of Osijek and with tanks on the other three sides, it must be frightening when guns shots can be heard around this area.

NUŠTAR   Early 1992 - 1993

We knew when we left Osijek that the village Nuštar was being heavily shelled but felt because of the places we needed to see we would still go on. We stopped at the hospital in Vinkovci to meet its chief to hear his story and take photographs. Things are grim but not nearly so bad as in Vinkovci. In Nuštar most people lost their lives mainly by the shells which created huge, in fact massive, craters. All homes completely devastated. I can only guess all these people are dead and died at the hands of an evil army. We heard when we got back to Osijek that this village was shelled again just after we left.

Nuštar

Monday, we went to Nuštar, the last village before the Croatian and Serbian border, utter devastation, no building was left standing but owners had trucks to go back. One old gentleman was trying to rebuild his ruined home. The shops were stalls on the side of the road and two remained open. A couple of old men were sitting on walls and half a dozen children running around. Took whole film and hope it is OK for showing everyone back home. I find this very hard to accept that men can do this to each other. I was told that in Vinkovci 5,000 people were killed, many taken away in lorries to be shot and then buried in communal mass graves.

During Monday night, I was awoken by shelling and explosions. I could hear the ta- ta-ta noise these things make. I felt great concern as to where it was, not for myself as I knew it wasn't in the next street. I heard next morning the road from Tenja 2 km away had been blown up by the Chetniks. (How these fanatics are feared by just everyone!) There apparently were three attacks.

The village I heard of at breakfast is now isolated and reports of more killings going on there and no one can get in or out! Just think of the terrible fear the people surrounded are in the grip of. Terrible, so frightening. There are few survivors from Vinkovci. Many who are left cannot accept their families are dead and refuse to stop searching for them.

On my return I must start an immediate collection for people here, money, clothes, food, whatever and also contact St Mary's re chairs!!! for spina-bifida children – so many items to ask for but all be provided of that I am sure.

The Royal Air Force in Quedgeley, Gloucester, had given me a hangar to store all the donations in. Amazingly, as fast as it emptied, it filled up again. There were so many willing hands to collect from schools, hospitals, churches and many, many individuals, so very many lovely people who cared and wanted to help in some way. Simply wonderful.

On my return home, I had to collect from a hospital in Truro as they had a surplus of items they could pass on to help Croatia. Gloucester Hospital gave tremendously and it was from here I bought so many paracetamol tablets. So many hospitals help and if they couldn't give what I needed, someone always told me who I should contact. Again, 'thank you' isn't enough to say.

PAKRAC AND LIPIK - GHOST TOWNS Early 1993

Pakrac is halfway between Zagreb and Osijek. I have found all streets and houses destroyed. It is horrific, a great shock. I truly didn't expect to see anything like this. The horrors of war I now understand, the shock of seeing

Pakrac

something like this was simply unbelievable. The people who lived here, those who were caught, shot and even tortured before their death must only have been filled with worst form of terror one can't even begin to think of. How they must have suffered. Every single house, in every street, every lane, even those far away from the rest, destroyed. Obviously systematically blitzed one by one, shelled and destroyed. There were mines still there, the obvious yellow tape and the warnings told us that. It was so sad to see pots and plants now dead around some of these houses, burnt out cars and even a wheelchair damaged and on its side in one driveway. Dogs were roaming around, and they could be heard barking in the distance. We had to stop at check-points, I think we must have caused quite a stir with our presence as suddenly VIP vehicles appeared from everywhere. To get to Zagreb from this ghost town we were quite clearly in some sort of danger from snipers for we were travelling alongside the Serbian border. With so much to consider our thoughts concentrated on the roads as we sped on our way.

Lipik

We could hear (Sunday) shelling and gun fire, still loudly going on in the village of Lipik. Today we visited the hospital here and spent time with the mothers group. How fortunate we were for just after we left the Chetniks shelled constantly this old and isolated village again, the mothers were safe, we heard later.

My thoughts of this trip are numerous. I am glad I came; my work with these refugees has now been confirmed to me as right. I have been shown the atrocities and the horrific damage of war and what it does. I can feel and understand more fully the terror and fear of these people as they fled to safety. Now there is nothing for these people to go back to and it will take a great many years to get even a glimmer of normality here even if this was stopped right now.

Too many homes gone, thousands of mines to be cleared. So many missing, probably dead and buried without the name of dignity. The land is so scarred, trees felled, farms blown to smithereens, the feeling of desolation is all around. But one must never give up on hope, for hope is in the future, for generations to come when they finally understand how so many suffered for democracy and peace. The hospital in Vinkovci will be for ever ingrained in my mind, the wickedness and evils of war almost bringing to the ground places for sick, a place of maternity and paediatric care as well as for the old and infirm. 95% of the windows were blown out, the mother and children's wards received a direct hit from the shells. Shrapnel scars are on all the walls, but still those doctors and nurses worked on and, strangely, in this place brought almost down to the ground the lighting and lifts still carried on working. May God bless each and every one as they bravely work on in this hospital which stands immediately on the borders and near the evil hands of the Chetniks.

On the way to Osijek we pass through beautiful countryside, again travelling through ethnically cleansed towns with totally destroyed houses blown up or burnt out. Those that weren't had huge holes in them, all looking dejected, a sad end making the whole area a huge graveyard. Even cars had been destroyed, such evil going on in this country.

I was able to cope with all of this when I got back home; my way of managing all of this horror was to talk about it in Churches, meetings, just tell everyone what was happening and, of course, I always talked about it to Our Dear Lord and Father, always.

DUHOVNA   STVARNOST 1995

Darko and I met Benjamin Mrkonjic from Grude, a town out in Bosnia. This man was put in a refrigerator for 24 hours, then was beaten and taken to a concentration camp. He lost more than half his weight, he had to dig with hands and was made to cut down trees. He was only given a small slice of bread to eat every day. Sometimes men were singled out to be shot, all were regularly beaten. When the Red Cross found this camp, he was told he would only have lived for another two weeks in those terrible conditions. His son is a doctor working on the front. He doesn't know where his other 16½ year old son is, or his wife and mother. When he was asked if there was hope for the future, this man had no words but broke down and cried. There are no dry eyes among us, our hearts went out to this poor man.

This afternoon, we went to the distribution centre to see the many stocks of goods, equipment, toiletries and soaps. There is so much there and it is very good to see it too.

We were taken to the Muslim Refugee camps. One, basic, was warm and quite clean with 300 people there, half of them children. The other had 3,000 people there and it feels difficult to understand how people have to live like this. There was no dignity in this camp, it was just squalid and I can only imagine rows of huts like this surrounded by mud can be no better than a concentration camp, the only difference being that the Muslims are not afraid of being hurt and being beaten by anyone here.

Dr Domas with his son Branko and Hazel

Today, Friday, we met Branko at Duhovna Stvarnost. He spoke of his first hand experiences of the terrible plight of the refugees. He spoke of the reasons and history of war and Croatia. He spoke about the religious aspect of this complicated country.

Friday afternoon to Duhovna Stvarnost. Saw refugees from Gradaćac (Bosnia), a town surrounded by the Serbian army. It seems Zagreb is now mainly helping Muslim refugees. They are in such a sorry state with a hopeless look in their eyes. There has been a lady refugee just sitting by the side of a fence in the centre of Zagreb since we arrived here. She doesn't seem to move, but her old face, wrinkled with age and the weather, creased into smiles when Steve gave her about £7.50 in Dinars. She put her hands together and thanked him. Steve, that act was so kind. He was one of the lorry drivers.

We thought we had found three little boys on their own yesterday and this caused us concern, but their families were nearby, they were safe.

Saturday – I am leaving for home back in UK. Will need many, many more items, clothes, food, just whatever I can bring back to help these people.

ZORAN FILIPOVIĆ 1991

Tonight, we are going to meet Zoran Filipović and have something to eat, so I will fill in the details on my return. We had decided tonight to leave here early Saturday morning. Strange how you meet people. I met Zoran Filipović on my first visit when invited to someone's home for coffee. Zoran is a very important photographer and journalist on all front line zones. He is the bravest man I have ever met. He confirmed all I thought that is happening here and was pleased for Andrew and his good Radio interview. (Andrew was from Radio Gloucester).

Zoran lived in Zagreb and that was where I met him. I found him interesting and very easy to talk to. He told me that he was known as 'The Panther'. I guessed that was because he worked at night. He mentioned that he went to the very front-line to check on family homes and that this was the area he 'rescued' people from. It would need stealth and bravery to venture to these places to 'save' people so it is easy to understand why he was known as 'The Panther'.

This is why I wrote a poem about him:

Zoran Filipović

Such sadness, sorrow and pain
Grief mixed with tiredness, deeply ingrained.
I see your eyes, your heart, in your mind
I see too much, would it better be blind?

Guns, shelling their blatant misuse
Cause heartbreak and terror, so many confused.
Then death, and maimed, create havoc in the mind.
When will this war end, can it be just in time.

My friend, take your pictures, record this all well,
Let future generations all know of this hell.
Then they too will learn and know of people like you
Who risk their lives in the work that they do.

Such sadness, sorrow and pain
Grief mixed with tiredness, deeply ingrained.
You love your country, man, woman and chid
But nothing can erase what I see in your eyes.

Hazel Hendry.

This could be for anyone in Croatia.

ŽUPANJA - JACOVAR - SLAVONSKI BROD 1992

Today, Tuesday, has been an exceptional day, spent at pharmacies in Županja, Jacovar and Slavonski Brod. What an experience. There was so little on the shelves, they had no money so couldn't buy anything to re-stock. I was taken to local chemists, similar to our own, but the same story everywhere, no money, no drugs, etc. to help people. The

Hazel with Darko Skugor and local police guards in Slavonski Brod

main pharmacy in Slavonski Brod, was a huge place that was totally surrounded by tree trunks to protect the windows and lower fronts of the buildings from shells and bullets. Empty cupboards, empty shelves, same story, even pharmacists are working for no money. The shelling and bombing, shooting and MIG attacks has only recently ended here and there is always the dread of other attacks especially as the Bosnian border is just over the river, clearly seen, houses devastated but Chetniks are there, even if they are invisible to the eye. Chetniks seem to be everywhere around here and into Nemenin, Osijek.

The hospital was the same terrible story. They are very worried for there is no money. This hospital has had a terrible time, over 10,000 operations in the weeks of war, shelled so badly there were 300 people lying on cellar floors. They need help here badly, so have a list of essential items needed urgently to collect when I get back home. They have given me a video which is not for the general public to see, only doctors, nurses, etc. I shall use this to raise money to help them. They gave me a tremendous welcome, a wonderful lunch and really would appreciate any help given to them.

Thursday, we went to see Milan and Jadranka. He is so very ill and is so obviously not going to be here much longer. I gave Jadranka last week £300 to pay for the costs of Milan's funeral for she hasn't any money at all. Will visit once again before I go back home. I saw Drago and shall be visiting his home on Sunday morning to meet his wife and sons again.

In the evening went to see people whose home is only 100 yards from the front line. Got out of the car and could hear the shooting immediately, apparently it had gone on all the previous night as well. They must get really frightened here they are so close the Serbs. These people are really friendly and with a great sense of humour. The usual food and wine flowed like water!

Friday, and today, we heard last night was bad for the people near Tenja (Tenja taken by the Serbs but this place is just on the verge of where we were last night). The Serbs were shooting at the Croatians all night and I have just been told it is far too dangerous for me to go to the very front line because of this.

Elderly woman waits for news of her son

Went to the Red Cross offices here in Osijek, people here are desperate for help so on my return am going to see if our local Red Cross can collect the things needed. They will send me a list of items during next week. I will speak to Peggy P when I get home. Hope very much that Zoran 'phones me for he is off to Sarajevo this weekend and things are much worse there now with the Bosnian Serbs being even more evil than ever

42

before. Heard today that Moslems are again attacking and torturing Croats, all parties are guilty of this but the Serbs are the real aggressors especially with the Chetniks fighting on their side. Such deplorable and ugly people in every sense of the word.

Saturday morning, and I stayed in bed until 6.45am. It normally is 4.30am, breakfast at around 5am with everyone starting work around 7am. Frano finishes work at 3pm. Kristina at 4pm. Marija, as she is a teacher, works shifts, either 8pm – 1 or 1-7 or 8. But this morning brought a lie-in! Then coffee and off to the market, a wonderfully interesting place, alive and full of activity, vivid colours everywhere. Meats, cabbage, lettuce, spring onions, lots of shades of green, bright red radish as big as plums, apples yellow, green and red. Lots of everything, clothes, leather, toys, records, books, everything, but at a big price, nothing is cheap and there is little money here as I have said over and over again. There are men on street corners, some leaning on doorway whispering quiet words as you walk by. I wondered for a while about these but quickly realised they would exchange any kind of money. Although strictly illegal and people being arrested from time to time these are the people to give you the best rate of exchange. I use them although the pound has not got the respect that the dollar has got. I got the best rate of exchange this week I have ever had, I felt very proud about this. Anyhow, back to my purchases. I bought two kilos of apples, two small green cabbages, one small carton of milk, and one small loaf and

I had to pay the equivalent of £5, and for people is Osijek that is a fortune to spend.

My overall impression of this area of Croatia is that it is much worse financially for people than when I first arrived here a few weeks ago. The lack of money has an effect on people, everyone the same, wanting to buy but cannot. Extremely worrying and I feel great concern and sympathy for every one of these people. I did make a discovery in Croatia though. Back home, I thought people more or less thought about things the same. I discovered that in other countries that isn't so, and I quickly learned to listen when spoken to very intently.

Whilst I was in Osijek, Marija had her 50th birthday. She taught English. She told me now I am old, here in Croatia when you are 50 things change. This made me realised that women who wore black were not only widows, but over 50. Such a shame to need to feel 'old'. Life is always worth living, age is a number. I really feel for the people in Croatia. They tell me I am like them, I understand, perhaps this is true. All I do know is I came and will never forget their suffering.

LASLOVO 1994

Hazel discussing future aid with local officials in Laslovo

On my first visit to Laslovo, when Darko and I were approached by two gentlemen (I do not know the names of these officials) to see who we were and what we wanted, we were told to only walk on solid ground because land mines were planted everywhere. These men took us to their train station, an innocent looking place. That was until a manhole was pointed out to us with its cover missing. We were told there were bodies down inside there.

Looking around this desolate place it seemed strangely odd to see fruit trees still standing, some even with fruit still on.

We were told, Darko and I, how so many people had been killed and nearly all properties blown up and destroyed.

It was no wonder we kept off the grass and we did stay on solid ground. Actually, it was always the better thing to do wherever we went.

Darko and I were the first people to get into Laslovo but this village desperately needed help.

I returned to Laslovo many times taking food, medical items, clothes, many items of furniture (given by Sue Ryder), bed linen, in fact everything that was needed. Never did I see too many people but there were men trying to rebuild their shattered homes. It was hard to realise that the next village was untouched but it was a Serbian village and it was there I was told most of their farming equipment was taken from Laslovo.

OTHER VISITS TO ŽUPANJA – VINKOVCI 1993 - 1994

The refugees here go to the Red Cross and similar organisations for food but like Zagreb they can only register for food at one centre. It has to be this way as there would be even more without food. People are selling their belongings to pay their bills, people can look but not buy, and, although soldiers are fed well, most look gaunt and under nourished. The problem will only get worse for even the government in Croatia is under great financial strain, they need help in this corner of Croatia, in Osijek, Županja, Jacovar, Vinkovci, Slavonski Brod. This area is badly overlooked and I wonder if maybe people are nervous of coming here.

Although I hear the powers that be in Serbia saying on TV that there is no war in Croatia, I ask them, 'Why, then, are Serbs still attacking near here at the very front line by Tenja? Why are explosions and shelling still happening in Županja, why is there still so much shooting going on near Vinkovci?' Even here, when walking, gun fire can be heard each and every day. People wonder and stop to listen even if a door is accidentally banged or something in the distance can be heard that is even slightly like an explosion. The people are generally nervous and under great strain. I was being taken to the very front line today but because of the attack by Serbs I have been told it is far too dangerous even for the soldiers, and they are only three or four miles away?

The children are regularly being checked by nurses specially picked for this work and are given special foods when children are found to be underfed simply because their parents have no money, and all refugee children are checked as soon as they arrive here. Everything is being done as far as humanly possible.

The hospital situation is grim, so utterly grim I just don't know where the surgeons, doctors and nurses are getting their strength from to go on working. To see how these places are supposed to survive is a shock to my system. Vinkcovci hospital is almost totally destroyed, defiant in its structure and solid in only its walls, underneath this mess in its basements and lower rooms. It is still functioning as a hospital should, and still the doctors and surgeons greet you with a broad and welcoming smile.

Osijek hospital is partly destroyed especially in the paediatric units and theatres with its glass windows all shattered and now in their places plastic sheeting is nailed instead of new glass for fear of further attacks in this part of the city. Certainly, not as bad as Vinkovci but still it has left its mark here.

Slavonski Brod hospital was amazingly missed by shells and gunfire in this town which has all its industry totally destroyed and many, just too many, of its houses brought to the ground. It is such a good thing this hospital wasn't too badly damaged for over 10,000 injured were taken there for surgery in six months, people lying in every conceivable place and many still there as their injuries were so horrific. How courageous and brave these people working here have been for whilst there was continual shelling from the Chetniks and Serbs just across the river (150 yards away), they never stopped working. One operation led to another. I can find no words to express how I feel about this situation here it is so very bad. This hospital has no money now to buy the drugs they need, no money for dressings and the threat from the Serbs and Chetniks just across the river is always there. Help must be concentrated especially for here, but help must be given to everyone is this forgotten corner of Croatia.

OSIJEK (MY MAIN TOWN) 1994

Sunday in Osijek was a very cold winters day and the morning has been spent with Darko and his family. Having lunch with them and going on later to Malica and Igor's (relations of Franco) country home for a barbecue. Another lovely day but as we are never left in the flat I had missed the telephone call from Zoran and also someone who phoned me from England about 100 blankets. I guess it is either Julie, Patsy or Pauline Hoffman.

Hazel in old Osijek

Sunday and this is my last day in Osijek. Marija came in with a cup of coffee at 7.30 am, very late to be getting up but things are more relaxed at weekends. I went out at 8 am with Kristina (Matusinović) to the market and a walk down

50

the banks of the River Drava. I have learned to really like this place of Osijek and feel so flattered people ask me to visit them soon and to even think about living here! They have said to me that I am one of Croatia, and I really take this as a great compliment.

Have been close of Tenja, Čepin to the refugee camp, Vinkovci to the hospital down to Županja where shelling has taken place which is close to Brecko on the Bosnian side which has been surrounded by Serbs and a town on the Croatian side where there has been a general alert because of shelling. Have also been to Slavonski Brod which is totally destroyed industrially with most of its houses gone through shelling. The bridge to Bosnia blown up as are the houses in Bosnia Brod the other side of the river. The Chetniks occupy a 12-mile stretch along here to Županja. Been near Đakovo, in fact I have travelled extensively around this corner of Croatia.

Monday, and this morning I am going to the refugee camp at Čepin. We were all up at 4.30 am with Frano leaving first and Kristina just leaving for work at 7.15 am.

The refugee camp, donated by German people, food etc. provided by Italians, is a sea of 300 prefabricated buildings, much smaller than our own 'prefabs'. In these houses there are three families. I went into one, there was a grandmother, two daughters, daughter-in-law and six children. Everything needed by these families is provided even down to knife and fork, and cup and saucer.

The refugees are encouraged to plough and develop a small piece of land between the prefab and in large squares. The purpose is to keep people busy and encourage them to grow their own produce, and it was obvious to see this is what the refugees want. I asked the family I spoke with about their needs, as they fled their homes at a minute's notice and no time to grab even a pair of knickers; it was clear they really did have a great deal of 'needs'.

They know there is no possibility of 'going home' as the Serbs have taken these and the refugees know they have been blown up. But they need to lean on charities for food, medicines and clothes. This need is urgent and will continue for a long while as there is little of anything here.

We went into the kindergarten, surgery and the store-rooms in this refugee village named, 'the village of friends'. Everyone seems happy (as happy as they can be under these circumstances!).

Somehow the people who had little before they lost their homes coped much better than those who once had been more 'well off'.

HELP FOR OSIJEK PRISON 1993
Worse than a Serbian Prison

It is quiet here in Osijek, no shooting, no shelling, just like being home in England, but just 35 miles away in Županja it is being bombed, and since arriving last Tuesday (now Saturday) there has been a 'red alert' attack there three times daily. The Serbs are attacking near Zadar and also Banja Luka in Bosnia and still attacking places like the Biriyas area. Karlovac has been bombed since my being here, as, too, has Gospic and Zadar. So, although it appears quiet here in Osijek that is not so, for all these attacks from Serbians can be heard here. I now feel when I return home, humanitarian aid should be collected and then given to Županja, Slavonski Brod for the hospitals and for Pozega here near Osijek.

There seems to be more available in shops for people to buy now, more food, more clothes, but I see people in the markets are not buying, just looking around at what is there. Most people have no money. I must also remember on my return here that artificial limbs are no longer required. I took a bread van filled to capacity with artificial arms and legs. Also had an arm made especially for a male prisoner in Osijek at the Chief's request, as this man worked in the kitchen. I was given 5 minutes to make some measurements but thank the Lord his arm fitted, he was given a cosmetic arm and a working arm by the kindness of a man who made prosthetics near to where I live in Gloucester. There is also a request for any medicines, tablets I can get too as well as dressings of all types, sutures, just anything I could get.

The officials in Osijek Prison were obviously deeply moved with the items I delivered for prisoners there. They were delighted too with all the pots, pans, cutlery and crockery that they received. One guard was so thrilled with what was given, he was grinning from ear to ear. You see, because of the generosity of the people back home, lots of prisoners now had shoes, clothes and many blankets to keep them warm as well as towels and toiletries.

I also met a young man who had been released from a Serbian prison who was in a very bad way. He showed me his back which immediately made me put my hand to my mouth as his back was covered in lash marks, huge red weals. An awful, terrible sight. How he must have suffered, such a wicked thing to do.

I was also told that some prisoners had their index fingers removed. This is a barbaric act and I am certain should never happen in any war, but, apparently every other man had the same treatment as well as being beaten.

To add more details: The man who was given the artificial arms was in prison for the murder of his wife. I was told that he and his wife were in a bad way about the war. So, he took a grenade to their bed, his wife died and he lost his arm. Now in prison with a working and cosmetic arm, I am sure these will help him in his future.

Some of the other prisoners I met there had deliberately committed crimes so they could end up in prison. It is important to remember many people lost everything in this war, but prison gave them food.

I do know they ate well because I was invited to the prison kitchen to share doughnuts they were making. Good ones too!

OSIJEK PRISON AND CHILDREN'S HOMES 1995

It was a cold winters morning on the Monday in 1995. This morning brought forth a visit to Osijek Prison. Here I am always made so welcome by The Governor who insists I have lovely food and a drink made by the prisoners. I asked about the man who worked in the kitchen who had two artificial limbs made and he is doing well and using his arm in all ways. He asked for all I could bring for their need was still great. Men are still arriving with few clothes and blankets are always scarce. Food is whatever is given and soap, etc. is always needed. These men may be in prison but they are human beings and should be treated the same as all others, so I help as much as I possibly can. I asked about prescriptions for the men and he gave me a pile to take back with me to see if help could be given this way. Hopefully, I may at least help some of them.

It was good later to walk around the market here in Osijek. I bought some tangerines, how fabulous they tasted. Later Dr Domac collected me to visit the home for retarded children. I was going to meet their parents too. I truly enjoyed being with them and it was wonderful to be asked to join them in eating pizza. On Monday, I have been invited to meet Mayor Kramarić. Dr Domac will take me for he has asked me to ask the Mayor to arrange extra rooms the children need; apparently he asked for them last year. Not sure if I should ask but I no doubt will!

Present from Pozega Prisioners

Tuesday has arrived and at 8am Darko and I will be on our way to Pozega prison. A police officer, 'Dario' is driving us there. I sometimes stayed in The Presidents holiday home at the prison, a really great house, very expensively furnished. I was there to see how I could help with aid on my next visit to Croatia.

In the evening Srećko Jelenić took me to see Igor (Igor is the young man blown up by a landmine and cannot move a muscle. He was a soldier clearing landmines from a house and there was a 'booby trap' which blew him up, damaging his body and brain in an extremely serious way). A group of people back home raised £3,004 for Igor by doing a sponsored workout and through their kindness and generosity I was to pass this money on to Igor. His parents were overjoyed and his mum cried for she couldn't believe people so far away would do this for their son. I was told Igor would be moved to Heidleberg to a Rehabilitation Centre to see if any help could be found for him.

(In fact nothing could be done and Igor was given a bungalow where he had medical staff looking after him. Igor died later with pneumonia).

Some of the items delivered to Osijek prison certainly helped the prisoners for they included boxing gloves, leather footballs, 50 mattresses, shirts, trousers, underclothes, shoes, one dishwasher, razors, soap, shampoos, washing powder, blankets and coats. They also received paracetamol which I could buy quite cheaply back in the UK.

Back at Osijek prison, the Governor met us (this time Marko was translating). I was told how the man in prison who got the artificial arms ended up there. Apparently he was in bed with his wife, pulled the pin out a grenade which killed his wife and he lost his arm. To die was something they both wanted. This is what war does to people. War is so evil.

In the evening I went to visit Marija Matusinović, It was good to see her for it was difficult to take in what had happened to this man and his wife I had been told about earlier.

I spent an hour-and-a-half with the Director of Klasje (children's home in Osijek). I came away with an endless list of requirements for the children. They need furniture for over 100 little ones, mostly orphans who have lost families in this way. Think I must contact Stroud News and Journal, the Citizen and Glos Radio for help with these things when I get home. URGENT.

The awaited phone call to see Major Kramarić and Dr Tibor Santo came at noon. He would like very much to travel to the UK to see Paddy Ashdown (I met Paddy Ashdown in Painswick) and David Heath (European Affairs) during the week of 26-31 October and to visit Painswick on 31st. And – fantastic – Dr Kramarić is going to help with the Retarded Children's Homes Request in Trolga.

After meeting with Igor's father to see how things are now, I had lunch with Darko and Drenka, and a meal in the evening with Dr Domac and his wife. These moments are so important for I learn what is happening in Croatia, what is needed and who and what is the most important.

AT LAST, SOME PRISONERS HOME 1993

Devastation in Vukovar

During the early visit to Zagreb, I met people who had fled from Vukovar and Nuštar. They all said how very much they wanted to go home. Vukovar, they never could as it is now a town of rubble, completely and utterly destroyed. Also, it is in Serbian hands. I have been told Serbian soldiers shoot on sight if anyone is caught taking photographs of what they have done to what was once a very beautiful town. Nuštar, not far from Vukovar, is now a ghost town. I have been there, as I have to Vukovar, taken photographs myself of every home shelled, many burned, all homes everywhere the same. There are no words to express how this makes one feel. It is just too awful, too dreadful, too shocking. I do not understand how man can do all these acts of violence.

On another occasion, when in Zagreb with more aid, a lady from the Red Cross arrived. She was extremely upset. She said that this evening 1,500 men were being released from

Samaritan International chairman greets released prisioners

Serbian prisons and she had no food or clothes to give them. From our aid she got as much as we had to give her. I saw these men as they arrived and I, like everyone else around, had tears running down my face. It was a pitiful sight. It would be so very good to thank each person in England who helped these people for it was only possible to help these men as it was through their kindness, thoughtfulness and generosity that these men had something. I was told later that it was only because of the lorries of aid arriving from the UK via me, that I was invited to be there. Prior to this, those invited had to wait in a hotel to receive a phone call. Then we would be told where to go to meet these men. It was 2am when the call came through. Waiting seemed like hours, but cars collected us (me and people from Zagreb and Osijek). I have no idea where we were driven to but it was in an army camp and we were taken to a compound next to the army hospital. It was very dark and it was explained to us that it had to be done this way because of the probability of snipers being in the hills around us. We were also warned it could be possible that snipers were in the coaches with the men about to be released, and that there could be bombs aboard the coaches too. As it turned out, no snipers, no bombs.

MASS GRAVES 1991 - ? (still being found in 2012)

I was told today of a funeral taking place in Tovarnika for 41 people. Their bodies had been found all together recently, in a pit. I was told they went missing in 1991 and had only just been discovered.

I am hearing all the time now of mass graves being found,

Why I must help Croatia

every one of them by being shot in the back of their heads. I was invited to the Mass. This lasted 2 hours. It was bitterly cold but still over 1,000 people were present to witness this. I didn't go to the Cemetery as I felt this was a private thing for families concerned. I wandered around Tovarnik to discover that it too had been extremely badly war-damaged and I can only imagine many more than 41 people had lost their lives here.

Sunday brought with it a restful day with a walk by the River Drava then lunch with Lyerka Koproicec and Pater Pero. It was good to find some peace here today, and enjoyable too.

Once, when I was near Osijek travelling with Darko, we went to a village near Jacovar. We stopped to talk to someone Darko knew and we were informed that two mass graves had been found. One had 200 bodies in it, the other 212. Constantly I heard about these graves and as I have already mentioned in the end over 1,300 were found in Croatia with the total far greater in Bosnia.

I thought of a graveyard in Osijek. It puzzled me why there was a lock on the gateway. Possibly it was to stop Serbs digging up the bodies of their families. I knew this happened when Croatian soldiers took back a village near Split. Near Split in the autumn of 1994, the Croatian Army took back a village being held by the Serbian Forces. I felt so proud of the Croatian Army when I read about this in a newspaper in Osijek. Milosovic ordered these people to go to Biriyas. The Serbian people dug up their dead relatives from burial sites and were ordered to return to Biriyas the other side of the river to Osijek. I remember seeing pictures of carts with these horror scenes in the same newspaper. Again, I was told it was an order by Milosovic. These people were unarmed, I was told.

FIGHTING IN THE STREET 1994

Saturday, was a day out in the country past Našice, a small Slavonian village, picturesque and quaint. It was an invitation to celebrate someone's birthday, it was for Lewis, brother-in-law to Elijah and brother of Marija. These people are rich, having lost nothing in the war, all in the family have jobs and not one of them lost any property. Hence there was lots of meat to be eaten, suckling pig, beef and various others. Piles of salads and many sweet cakes, all to be washed down with ever flowing bottles of local wine and beers. Eating started at 10.30 am when we arrived and continued until we left at 6.30 pm. For Julia and Ali to celebrate their wedding, they send a bottle of plum brandy, made from the fruit of their trees. We all arrived 'home' very tired and very full.

During the night in the Spring, there was lots of noise and once I heard loud banging noises. When I went on the balcony to see what was happening, there was a man banging another man's head heavily on the flag stones. He then started kicking the man in the head and top of his body. I woke up Marija and Frano but they were not interested and this morning Marija told me they didn't want to telephone the police and anyhow they were probably 'only two drunks'. Even so, I was very worried for the man being hit.

Help is needed here but a lot can be given through the Red Cross, but I must employ the use of a church and its congregation when I get home to get a huge supply of food and soap, etc. There is such a lot to get done on my return home but I am so very pleased it has been possible for me to visit so many ignored and neglected places here in this north/east corner of Croatia.

Wednesday, and today is to be a quiet day. I 'phoned Patsy in UK and also Jadranka to see how Milan is. Poor Milan, so very ill with cancer, is still holding onto life. I had a telephone call from Zoran. He is to go to Sarajevo tomorrow. He plans on meeting the powers that are there, then he is travelling on to Zepa and Goražde to get some of his friends out. So brave is this man, his only thought is for his country and countrymen, his own safety is the last thing he thinks about.

Thursday, and I forgot to mention, yesterday was the first time I went into a Catholic church to pray, and I prayed for Zoran and his safety. Today I am going to the Ivan Filipović school to see an English class taking place, then, at 11 am I am going to Osijek Hospital to meet the soldiers who were so seriously injured in Zadar.

The Ivan Filipović school were so very pleased to have an English person in their classes to speak to, to hear such very sensible questions about Osijek, humanitarian aid, schools, fashion, sports, and languages. Such lovely children aged between 10-15 years old, and if penfriends can be found, they would be delighted. 800 pupils there, in all. One of the children here said I must be very rich to do all this work for Croatia. I said, no, I wasn't rich but had been given a job to do as a Christian. I also told the children it was people in the United Kingdom who gave these things. I only delivered them.

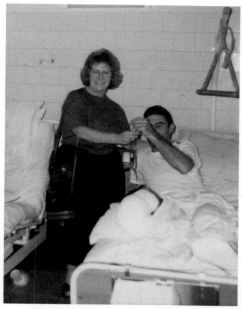

Hazel receiving crucifix

We went to Osijek hospital where Marija's sister is a sister-in-charge of the men's surgical unit. I met the men who had been injured at Zadar last week, three with parts of their legs missing, all looked ill and pale. One gave me his Croatian emblem attached to his crucifix. I gave him the one Penny (a friend in UK) gave me, it was a beautiful, very heavy silver one, as I understood what it meant for him to give me his.

Marija told me there were only four pairs of scissors in the whole of her unit, everything went with the war. I was given a complete list of things so desperately needed. The soldiers spoke of the urgent need of metal detectors to search for mines to stop children and adults from losing their limbs. (I wasn't allowed to bring these).

I forgot to mention that last night there was a heavy exchange of shell and gunfire between Serb and Croatian forces. It went on for at least an hour and a half. Also I am unsure if I mentioned the Orthodox church which was blown up by Serbs last Sunday, an almighty explosion which was followed by another as the planned demolition of the bridge went ahead.

The hospital at Osijek had its basements crowded with people waiting to register to be admitted into its wards. Soldiers on crutches, civilians on stretchers and chairs, there must have been over one hundred people there.

Last evening there was an attack – a general alert – by Serbs on a village near Jasenovac. There is supposed to be a cease fire, laughable really, especially as one hears on the news that all is quiet on the Croatian fronts. People are questioning why fourteen Serbia tanks are being allowed to stay in a village near Vinkovci whilst Russian UN peace forces are there seeing what is happening. Serbs attacking Brcko just across the River Sava, already they have taken half but are fighting here badly in Bosnia, only a stone's throw from the Croatian border.

DARKO, FRANO AND MARIJA 1992

Frano Matusinović

Sunday, I was pleased to arrive in Osijek to be met by Darko, Marija and Frano, it was really good, and were they surprised at the size of the lorry! We parked the lorry at the back of the pharmacy which had a man to watch it overnight. We then went back to eat and talk, it was really so very good.

On Monday morning we all arrived at the pharmacy to see about 20 people waiting to help unload. Everything was sorted into separate heaps and clearly labelled as to who they were to be delivered to. The newspapers and radio were there to interview and everyone was so happy to receive all these things from the people in Gloucestershire. After the interviews we went and delivered the beds, etc. to the Osijek hospital and met the chief in charge of the hospital who I gave £600 to. He gave me a certificate, a really nice one in a cover which had a map of Osijek on it.

It was weird for me on Monday night when Marija and I walked along the Promenade by the River Drava, we could hear the shooting across the river but we both kept on walking and talking. This made me realise how easy it is to accept what is happening and just carry on the normalities of life. We did decide to walk back though for the shooting continued for quite a long time. She thought the village of Baranja (just across the River Drava) was under fire.

The children's homes here in Osijek are being organised and run to the best ability of very well-trained young

Orphans in Osijek

people who have a great love and give tremendous care to children who have very little. One home I went into Dječji Dom Klasje has 140 children to care for. Most have no parents, some had one who is so poor it is impossible to care for the child or children, so they come into the home and see the children whenever it is possible. It has to be remembered that to be poor here before the war was bad, to be poor during the war is utterly deplorable and it must be similar to walking in a field of mud and not being able to reach the sides. Just so very terrible for them. This home is full of great compassion, and they (the helpers) are given small groups to care for, 10-15 in a group. They then only care for this little group. The children are from birth to 20 years, but their needs whilst here are immense and just everything is needed from clothes, to food, to furniture, but they say 'please no money, only things for the children'.

Then there is the kindergarten with the disabled children and the little blind girl. She is 4 years old, has a tumour on her brain and needs surgery urgently and quickly. I must speak to Peggie and Patsy when I get home to see if they can contact a neurologist I could perhaps contact to get help for this dear little girl. Unfortunately, this little girl died before anything could be done for her.

The Ivan Filipović school was thrilled and delighted to get the clothes from Dean Close School. I must contact them on my return to see if more is available for there are 800 pupils at this school including 120 refugee children.

I also spent time at a detention centre for young people, those between 10 and 20 years, some sent by the courts for minor offences. Most have behavioural problems, all seem to have emotional problems and each of them having difficulty with coping with the war. It was interesting to be taken around this school for it reminded me so much of The Lar Childrens home in Portugal. Although the Government help support this centre there isn't enough money for things such as carpets and curtains.

Friday evening was spent at the home of friends to Marija and Frano, their names escape me for I have difficulty in remembering Bosnian, Croatian and Muslim names as they are so different from ours, but I do remember their son's name – Dalibor. We had a typical Bosnian meal, a lovely evening, eating outside on the patio. Children could be heard playing but the firing of guns let us know were only 150 yards from the front line. Before I return home I have been invited back here to a barbecue.

Saturday, what glorious day. From leaving Osijek at 8 am we went 'to the country' to Milica and Iver's country home. A chalet set in grounds of lawns, fruit trees, a very large pond and even fished on here catching two fish, a beautifully blossomed orchard spanning out to a field in which potatoes were being planted. Such a lovely day, no guns blasting until around 5pm, when they could be heard. The sun shone and when leaving at 7pm, everyone had a shining, healthy glow. Just lovely.

There was much to do during the day, weeds to be pulled, pansies to be planted, lawns to be mown, grass to be raked up. I had a wonderful time. So much food, fish soup cooked in a huge cauldron to be followed by chicken, barbecued and with huge hunks of fried bread and freshly picked spring onions. The pudding was similar to strudel but very much sweeter; so much so, the sugar was crunchy. Beer and wine was taken whenever the sun made one need it, and it did!

Sunday was another day of visiting, it was important to visit Županja for the shelling here has been heavy even up until 5 days ago. It is on the edge of Bosnia where the Chetniks are grounded. Once they got in Županja and even on to the roofs of Marija's brother's house. Marija's parents' house was the first one to be shelled in Županja collapsing the whole front of their home. The second shell was to totally destroy her aunt's house which was at the bottom of her parents' home. So much for 80 year- olds to cope with. (This town surprisingly seemed to be one of affluence, not like Osijek, a town that is fighting to survive). It had its buildings surrounded by trees protecting the windows and doorways from the onslaught of grenades and shells, but it also had cafes with music blaring and people sitting outside on white chairs around bright red tables, sipping their coffee. One has to admire people over here, surrounded by all this danger and they carry on as normal until a general alert is heard, then they have a scatter to comparative safety.

We visited Marija's parents' home to have lunch. This lovely old lady cooked the most delicious food, we had a kind of sliced meat with spring onions, apple and bread to start with, chicken, cauliflower, chips and salad to follow, then homemade pastry and biscuits to follow. So much food all cooked by this lovely old lady. There seemed to be something in my hand to eat or drink the whole time there. Their home was typical Croatian, long and low, one room leading to the next. Past the house the poultry pens, and then packed and neatly hoed gardens onto the orchard with trees blooming full of pear, apple and plum blossom. Sheer joy and not a gunshot to be heard.

When we left here we visited Marija's brother's house, a really lovely one which appealed to me. Chalet styled with teak panelled walls instead of wallpaper, lovely cotton curtains, crisp and white, but to show war is not far away where the windows were shattered, green mesh is covering the spaces where glass should be. Again food was offered but although the banana, chocolate and nut cake made my mouth water, I stuck to accepting an apple and politely but firmly refused to have coffee.

The garden was undamaged by the war and the lilac and magnolia trees were in full bloom. These together with all the other colourful shrubs glowed as the sun shone on to them. It is hard to believe that in a few weeks the sun will be so very hot here that the shrubs and grass will be a scorched brown colour, but people assure me this is just how it will be.

We left this delightful house and home to visit friends of Frano's, another pharmacist who works with Frano, whose husband is the local vet. Like Frano and Marija, they live in a flat, and again like them, near the top. It was full of green plants and on the walls lots of pictures painted by a local man. Again, drinks were offered and I had possibly the best cup of coffee since arriving here, a big cup, not too strong and floating on the top lovely frothy beaten cream. We left here quite soon as Frano wanted me to meet his aunt who is a Dalmatian lady.

Her house was right on the edge of Županja, edging onto the forest with only one other tiny house and a field keeping it away from whatever might be inside it. A tiny house, a poor lady who had obviously had a very hard and busy life. She has a deep brown, weathered skin, and glistening white teeth. She is tiny but her arms so muscular and hands so overworked, their skin hard and tough. She is wearing black and only took off her scarf when I asked if I could take her photograph. When we arrived, she was just about to have coffee and pancakes. With her was a friend, a peasant lady but Croatian and broad and sallow skinned, but both shared that hard working look.

I accepted a fruit drink and when we left, even though she was so poor, Marija took home eggs, lettuce, spinach and spring onions.

As we were leaving I took a photograph of the hens and cockerel for they had been given their own little 'road' to walk along between the lawn and next garden.

Poultry Pen

Eventually we got back home at 9-ish and it was so good to talk for a while with my own lovely daughter back home in London.

Monday, and I cannot believe I have been here a week and 2 days, and that in a couple of weeks I'll be on my way home. Time goes so quickly.

It's to be a quiet day catching up on this journal though I have spoken on Radio Gloucestershire to tell people back home how things are and stopped to have coffee and a chat with one of Marija's colleagues. Poor Frano is ill in bed with the flu. (This writing business is very tiring!!).

THE MATUSINOVIĆ FAMILY

Last night we, the Matusinović family and myself, went to Dario's agricultural home – I had been there on a previous visit to Croatia – spent a lovely evening with his family laughing, talking, having a drink and watching TV. It seems strange visiting this home in Tenja for their garden is literally next to the frontline and with Chetniks only less than a mile away. Life has to go on for Dario and his family and they were digging their back garden when we arrived. The last time I was here was in December and there was continual machine gun firing all the while, but last night we heard one shot and thought maybe someone had shot his supper. Marija is not well, her ears are causing her great discomfort and being there this time made me feel uncomfortable. I had been staying there but they asked me politely to stay elsewhere in future as the war and its toll had been too much for her. I thanked her and Frano for their past kindness and said I understood. It was not a problem.

Frano was the chief pharmacist and I sent medication to him to be sent out to those who needed help. But I went to the pharmacy yesterday and noticed 10-15 boxes I had delivered there the previous evening were missing. I did not feel happy about that because only people in the pharmacy could have removed them. No one owned up.

This morning I walked along the promenade of the River Drava with Kristina, a very beautiful day, warm and it is the first day of Spring here. It was lovely to see men and children fishing, just enjoying themselves. Kristina looks lovely and more at peace with herself than on previous visits. We had walked along here several times on other occasions as it was so very good to feel the cool air on my face and to hear the movement of the water in the river.

Left for the pharmacy at 6.50pm to sort out donated drugs, medicines, etc. - these will be shared between Osijek, Županja and Vinkovci hospitals. Local doctors will use these to help their patients.

Darko (Skugor, my translator) looked tired. Baby Filip had to go into hospital on Saturday as his temperature had reached 40 degree. As there was no bacteria present, Drenka and Darko were told it was virus. Baby Filip is only a few weeks old. It is no wonder his parents looked so tired.

Maria returns to teach at her school today; she teaches English. Still looks unhappy and miserable with herself but her ears are improving.

Slavonski Brod: people still need things here, so many made homeless and 95% of industry destroyed. Must bring clothes, blankets, shoes and food for Slavonski Brod on my next visit to Croatia.

Slavonski Brod Bolnica (hospital) urgently need x-ray plates and drugs – must speak to Jonathon Unwin at Gloucester Royal when I get home and also John Hubbard. <u>URGENT</u>.

Sandbags in Vinkovci Hospital

Today, Wednesday, am now waiting to visit Vinkovci and its frontline devastated hospital. This is a hospital which all doctors except one, Dr Domas, had run away from, for Serbs had killed most of the patients and ransacked the hospital. I can understand this for they must have been terrified. (I was told later that most doctors were, in fact, Serbian).

THE JELENIĆ FAMILY

Professor Dr Srećko Jelenić and his wife, Dr Zvonka were two people who invited me into their home with open arms. Srećko was a lawyer who went on to be a judge in The Hague (I mentioned this previously), and, Zvonka was a dentist. They have two sons. Ivica is the older one and Zvonimir the younger. Ivica is a lawyer like his father. Their home was in central Osijek within a delightful avenue which had small trees every now and again set along the footpaths.

They were kind, thoughtful and caring people with a complete love for their country Croatia. They invited me in for meals, introduced me to many interesting people, Pater Pero Mihic, being one. Pater Pero was to introduce me and direct me to where children were in need, sometimes desperately. It was good to be able to give a multitude of items to help his work with children.

It was amazing how Our Lord placed people in this work so that it would be successful. I remember when I spoke to Our Father, telling him I would do this work and that He must provide all that was needed; and he did in a magnificent and fantastic way.

It would be wrong to write these journals and not to mention people like Darko Skugor and Srećko and Zvonka Jelenić. There were so many individuals to thank in Croatia but these people stood out in making and doing this work for Croatia so successful. I thank them deeply and with love. These people are still my great friends.

THANK YOU

Taking humanitarian aid to suffering in The Balkans, mainly in Croatian side, Osijek, Čepin, Županja, Vinkovci, Slavonski Brod, Pakrac and Lipik during the last seven years has changed me more than I can say. The war has been a shocking, painful experience and the aftermath too painful to bear for these poor people now have to re-build their lives, the majority without senior members of their families to help.

I have taken all types of aid over to help, all (mostly) from all over our country for the hospitals, children's home, refugee camps, schools, prisons; just anyone in need has been helped wherever, whenever possible with whatever people have asked for. The vehicles to take aid to Croatia are expensive. This money has to be raised and so far 38 lorries filled to capacity have gone to Croatia.

So many lorries to follow. When George Hoffman said, "Hazel, the people in Croatia need your help", I sat and spoke to Our Lord and I said I would do it but He must give me all that I would need for this work. And He did in great abundance. Thank you Dear Father.

Once when speaking at Malmesbury Abbey about this work, I told how gifts, however or whatever they were, all were needed now and would be in months to come in great abundance. The Abbey supported this work greatly and this was tremendously encouraging for me. After one service, a young man came up to me. He didn't actually speak but put an envelope in my hands, no name, no address. In the envelope there was £1,000. An overwhelming act and so very generous, and so very kind.

Everyone knew the costs of lorries and what I had in requests (many) from many whilst in Croatia, and it was through people like this young kind man that this 'His work' was successful.

DONATIONS FOR HOSPITALS 1998

I left for Croatia on January 26th, having in mind to visit as many of the places I normally try to get to. Two doctors kindly collected me from the airport in Zagreb and then drove me to Osijek. Charming people who really wanted to help in some way.

Dr Srećko Jelenić (Professor of Law and a Judge later in The Hague) has made a flat available for me which is warm and has all I need in it. It is central in Osijek which is really good.

After a good night's sleep I contact Frano Matusinović and Darko Skugor (a pharmacist, translator, driver and a very good friend) to make plans for the short time I have here. Before moving from Osijek, I called into Klasje, a children's home, to say I would be there later. On Thursday, I met up with Frano, Darko and Dr Domac (a vet) to make arrangements for me to visit a 'club' for retarded children. I look forward to this as I find all these children delightful and I also look forward to seeing the work they are encouraged to do. Frano took me to Vinkovci hospital to see Dr Dolanski and find out how he can be helped on the next visit with aid.

Today is Friday and Darko is taking me to Slavonski Brod where aid I have on this visit with medical and surgical items is going. Have to give great thanks to EMS Medical in Stonehouse, Gloucestershire for all of their many donations. All other aid on this visit, food, toiletries, blankets, furniture – yes, even that – and clothes for men, women, children and babies.

Also, Pater Pero Mihic is awaiting for baby items – he takes care of 1,000 mothers and babies in Osijek and its areas. He will collect these things off the lorry as they are so desperately needed. So many helping so many more in times of need. May Our Lord bless them all.

These are some of the donations given to me to take to hospitals so desperately in need:

Binoculae microscope (3 pieces). Olympus BX40.
Fibre bronoscope. Olympus. Wolf. Storz.
Colonoscope for Gynaecology.
Anaesthetic machine with ability ventilation for patients;
Dressings, bandages, needles 2.5-10.
Surgical gloves.
Uniforms. Doctors coats. Theatre gowns. Green cloths.
Soap. Toiletries. Chairs (special needs).
Metal boxes full of surgical instruments.
Bed linen. Blankets.
Blood Pressure gauges. Mortuary trolleys.
X-ray films and plates.
The lists I delivered were endless.

During this time, donations initially were kept in tents in my garden but it soon became obvious that much greater space was needed. The RAF in Quedgeley, Gloucestershire very kindly offered me a hangar to store everything in. The aid I wanted to collect mainly was medical and surgical equipment and medication of all types (including artificial limbs). Also food, as much as I could get. These came in abundance from all over the UK, there were toys from France and Spain, money from France and the UK.

There was an abundance of toys, clothes, bed linen, mattresses, food, toiletries, simply everything we all need to survive on. There were all types of hospital equipment given, sheets, blankets, swabs, needles, the list is endless.

How Our Lord helped in this, His work. So very many individuals to thank, so very many kind and generous people have helped in this work. So many just 'dropping things off', delivering or filling up the lorries. The Sue Ryder organisation gave so much furniture. This did help us so very much. A huge and heartfelt thank you to everyone who did anything to help the people in Croatia. May Our Dear Lord and Father Bless you all.

MATTHEW BIGWOOD 1996

25TH March, and I am taking a news reporter from the Citizen in Gloucester over to Croatia. His name is Matthew Bigwood. We arrive in Osijek via Zagreb very early in the morning feeling very weary as it was a long journey. After a good night's sleep, Darko collected me from the flat I was in and then we went and collected Matthew from where he was staying. Darko decided to take us to places where he felt Matthew could do his work as a reporter. We went to Vinkovci and Ernestinova. I think the Serbs must have stayed in this village because it was very noticeable that properties were still standing, whilst in the village of Laslovo next door, they were utterly devastated. Every home, every street absolutely everywhere, not one building left standing.

Laslovo

I became involved with Laslovo when Darko suggested he take me there but warned me it was extremely dangerous and we would need to be careful. So, we went, and on arriving we saw two gentlemen walking towards us, they looked concerned and asked why we were there. Darko told them. They then relaxed and turned to me and gave me the biggest hugs I ever had. These men were looking for graves of people missing. They had found the body of a 26-year old man in a shallow grave (they knew who he was). Another grave was found to be emptied of two bodies – (26- and 29-year old soldiers). No coffins found, no bodies, only coffin handles. Eventually a mass grave was found not far from here. The two officials asked if I could get furniture, seeds, food, clothes, bed linen etc.etc., the list was endless. This request is extremely urgent and I must act on this as soon as I get home. They told us a few people had returned and were attempting to rebuild their homes but had nothing to go in them. Matthew and I came back to my flat to wait for Drenka and Filip to arrive. Whilst waiting, Srećko Jelenić arrived with a message from the Children's Home that they would collect their aid tomorrow.

Took Matthew to meet Dr Domac and to hear about the work going on for the Retarded Children. He gave Matthew an invitation to go and see the children at their work.

Friday. Called into Klasje (the Children's Home) for Matthew to take photographs of the children and where they live. I never stop thanking Darko for being always with me for without him it would be very difficult. Sometimes I understand what people are saying but I cannot speak in their language to hold a long conversation. I took Matthew for a two hour walk around Osijek through the old town of Osijek named Tryja (it had been badly damaged with shell-fire). Later, we had a meal together and Matthew went back to the hotel.

Saturday. We went back to Laslovo to the funeral of the young man found in the shallow grave. Over 1,000 people turned up. Heard today of more mass graves being found near Vinkovci, one had over 200 bodies in it. How can a person do this I cannot understand this, such dreadful, evil people. During this event, Mario, a family friend of Kristina, met up with us. He took me and Matthew to see the "rat hole" he was in during his soldiering time. It really was a "rat hole" dug inside a ditch. He said at nights when he was there, rats ran over him.

Saturday. Lunch at Dr Dalibor Koprolćec's home today. Matthew was shown a film of the start of the war in Osijek. I was glad to get back to the flat for I had started a cold.

Monday. I am staying in the flat today, cold not good. Matthew is going with Darko to meet at Caritas, then meet up with Dr Domac for him to see the children at work in their school.

PS   Matthew stayed a week in Croatia and I have to say thank you for such a wonderful report he made in the local Citizen paper. It was really good.

THE NUNNERY Summer 1997

It all seems much quieter in Croatia now that the war and all its horrors have moved on to Bosnia. But that doesn't mean that shelling or gunfire with snipers still around has all stopped. No, it's all still as dangerous to be in Croatia as it always has been since starting Our Lord's work over here. It is impossible to walk on grass anywhere; it is safer to walk on hard surfaces for landmines in all shapes and sizes have been left everywhere by the Serbian Chetniks. It is much more dangerous around Vinkovci, Nuštar and places like Ernestinova and Slavonski Brod. In Slavonski Brod, gunfire can be heard still every single day and I am still being told that I must 'watch my back'. In Osijek, there are more and more people milling around the market. There is a desperate lack of money, so people generally just look. I heard a woman screaming that someone had taken her money. I felt so sorry for her, I really did.

I remember a different type of quietness. Pater Peter Pero said I had been invited to a Nunnery as they too had 'things' they needed. I cannot remember where it was only that it had a beautiful landscape and wooded areas around it.

I went with Pater Peter and Srećko Jelenić, and we arrived at a heavily gated building, its gardens immaculate but nevertheless it was all very quietly beautiful.

It was an Order of Silence, with only a few nuns permitted to speak to us. We saw few novices, but were told there were 19 in all. We were shown around this nunnery but were also shown where we couldn't go. Along some areas there were grids and we couldn't go beyond these either. It was so peaceful, absolutely lovely, with a magnificent Chapel, but the main door was locked behind us and all windows beyond reach and closed.

We had a simple, but delicious, meal together and produce provided by the Nuns themselves. We stayed just a couple of hours. I left them with some money as I couldn't see how else I could help. I said a quiet prayer for these ladies who have shut themselves away from the world. I remember saying to Srećko, "Don't leave me here"!

A NEWSLETTER

I always sent out newsletters so that people would always know how their monetary donations were being used and also to pass on more news they all needed to hear.

Request for prayer, aid and Christmas gifts for children

Please pray for this peace to continue it is all so very fragile over there.

As I have mentioned poverty is still very obvious and made worse by this war. Caritas has a kitchen in Osijek and they feed over 1,650 people every day. Getting the food is a very serious problem for Caritas for there is always a heavy shortage of it.

I need bedlinen, clothes, shoes, FOOD OF ALL TYPES, toiletries, small furniture, carpets, cups & saucers, plates, cutlery, glasses, in fact everything we need to make our homes function normally are still urgently needed. I cannot stress enough THE AID IS STILL URGENTLY AND DESPERATELY NEEDED with so many people still suffering, so many homes needing repairs and, when people are able to return to their homes there will be no money to help them get back to normal. Many of those who have returned to their shell-destructed homes are finding out how difficult it is to manage without sufficient KUNA in your pocket.

I plan to make the next visit at the end of November and hopefully take two lorries over there again filled to capacity with the things they need. This will be the Christmas trip and once again I have names of children needing Christmas gifts and, as in previous years, everything to make a happy party for at least some of them. Should you like names,

Hazel with Christmas Gift Donations

please contact me on (*old number*). I can only say that one small gift will make one little person extremely happy. Thank you so much for making this possible.

I have been approached by another hospital for help, more help requested by another Priest and again by more war disabled and by people who are diabetics. I have visited even more homes with children now orphans and to schools still doing the best they can with very little to work with.

Nevertheless, thank you for all the efforts made to make these sad lives happier. They thank you for this so very much and please continue your PRAYERS, people in SLAVONIJA send their greetings to everyone.

With love, and God Bless you.

Sincerely, Hazel

ANOTHER NEWSLETTER

Fax from Hazel Hendry

Dear Friend

Friday the 13th September took me once again to Osijek to deliver from two 39 tonne lorries the much needed humanitarian aid again donated by so many caring people. A sincere THANK YOU to everyone who gave in whatever way, you are all fantastic in your collecting and giving. Now I have actually forgotten the exact amount of aid sent over but the value has been estimated at over 4 million pounds and the last vehicles leaving the UK made it the 30th trip, and, I think, my 26th, but this is not important.

An aid lorry near Hazel's home

It was so lovely travelling by night over there for all the places I mention to you look similar to home with their street lights twinkling with an abundance of traffic travelling everywhere without fear of being stopped. Homes seemed to be getting back to some kind of normality although there is great evidence of poverty, lack of furniture, money, clothes, food, equipment to repair homes, in short these people are still suffering in shocking and dreadful ways. Lots of things are being repaired, for example, drains, roads, sewers, gas pipes and such like are obviously top of the list where priorities go. But it is lovely to be aware of peacetime with only the occasional gun shot and only once did we hear what was obviously a shell exploding, that could have been one left carelessly in the ground and some unfortunate animal found it.

PRESENTATION OF PAUL HARRIS AWARD FROM ROTARY CLUB OF STROUD

"Representatives of Stroud Rotary Club are especially pleased to be here tonight.

Peter Hewins a Stroud Rotarian who sadly died earlier this year kindly left the Club a sum of money which was to be donated for charitable purposes. Peter supported Hazel for many years and was our link with her for the many trips she has made in providing aid to Croatia.

On Peter's behalf and Stroud Rotary Club would like to present you with a cheque for £1,100. I understand this will allow you to take a second lorry with aid and Christmas gifts on the trip you are shortly to make.

I am sure that everyone here is very privileged to know Hazel and can only marvel at the tremendous work she carries out in getting aid to those that need it.

Last year, Stroud Rotary Club recognised this contribution by presenting her with the Paul Harris award. This is the highest award that Rotary can make and it was sanctioned by Rotary International based in America to show Rotary International's appreciation of her work. As we are in the company of her many friends and supporters tonight, we thought it would be a good opportunity to present the award."

THE ROTARY FOUNDATION OF ROTARY INTERNATIONAL

Hazel Hendry

is hereby named a

PAUL HARRIS FELLOW

in appreciation of tangible and significant assistance given for the furtherance of better understanding and friendly relations among peoples of the world.

I was given a medal. Peter was a lovely, kind man and I had no idea about this which he had planned. It was always surprising for me to get awards. They were something I didn't expect or thought I could receive. At the end of this work given for me to do, I actually received over 50 written awards, some or should I say many, extremely beautiful, many from Croatia and some from the UK.

SOME THOUGHTS BEFORE NEXT VISIT
November-December 1996

Friday 25th   Lorries load and leave Gloucester for Croatia

Tuesday 29th   Hazel leaves for Zagreb, then train journey across Croatia to Osijek

Wednesday 30th   Lorries arrive Osijek
One to leave immediately for Županja and then on to Vinkovci Hospital.
Unload and return to Osijek

Thursday 1st   Second lorry unload, Osijek Prison.
Slavonski Brod and Vinkovci Children's Homes – these to be delivered by local men from Pharmacy.
Home where little blind girl is.
Finally all party gifts etc., food, clothes, blankets for Home by Pharmacy.

Monday 5th   Prepare room for party

Tuesday 6th   5.30 pm. Party at Children's Home

Any free time to retrace steps along front-line to Children's Homes, Hospitals, refugee camps, prisons, churches to find out what is needed for next delivery.

Monday 19th   Home

CHRISTMAS AND OTHER GIFTS 1997

I put out an appeal for Christmas gifts for children who would not get even one gift, simply because people needed food and there was little money for that.

Gifts from Horsley School for Croatian Children

The response was amazing. I thank the Lord continually, for after George Hoffman said to me, "the people of Croatia need your help", I prayed hard and said, "Well, I asked Our Lord for Him to provide all I would need so that I could do his work well". And He did, by spreading His Hands all over the UK thereby opening people's hearts for this great need, the workings of Our Dear Lord and Father are truly amazing. When gifts came there was enough to fill two of the largest lorries from Croatia. Enough gifts to send over one vehicle to Osijek and the other to Pozega. Such a wonderful Christmas for the many orphan children and for those desperately poor families in Croatia. Thank you Lord.

The Red Cross in Bristol generously gave an ambulance filled to capacity with dressings, swabs, bandages, blankets, towels and many items beside these. It was a large item to give me to take to Croatia so I contacted TEARFUND and they then contacted Samaritans Purse who then delivered it to Croatia. When in Zagreb sometime later, I decided to call into Samaritans International to see if the ambulance had arrived there. The complex the Americans had there was very well thought out by having sections around a central point above these sections which would make it easier I guess to see what was going on all around. Anyhow, I was directed to a lady in this 'tower', asking politely if she knew if the ambulance had arrived. She said, 'what do you want to know for?' I explained all, then she replied, 'it's in Bosnia' – then walked away.

People in the United Kingdom are amazing people, they continually hold sales, sell books, collect and give all these items which go out to help a country crying out for help. Not only do people collect all types of clothing but the donations of good food and much needed toiletries they generously give too. Ladies sent loads of sanitary wear as these were not available for a great many during this war. One lady rolled up newspaper because there was nothing else. Lord, your fingers spread out all across our country and people feel and give because of this. Thank you, Dear Father.

People in France sent Teddy Bears. I have received money from Spain and the United States. Ladies from Scotland made and delivered to my home many baby clothes. Thank you just doesn't seem enough.

AND FINALLY 2012

Things are getting quieter now and although I keep 'putting my foot in the door', I know our Lord and Father is telling me it is time to stop. So hard and difficult for me after all I have shared with so many. It is getting more difficult to raise money for the lorries and I am aware that there are so many others in the world who need help. After sending a further two vehicles with aid, my work for my Lord and Father has finally ended. I have only praise and thanks to Him for giving me this work to do. He simply used my hands.

Srećko and Zvonka Jelenić

And finally – a few years ago, I received an invitation to the wedding of Ivica Jelenić, son of Professor Srećko Jelenić and his wife, Zvonka. I went, and it was a wedding I have never seen before. 750 guests with celebrations over a weekend. A magnificent experience.

Whilst there, the Croatian Army heard of my visit and after contacting me I was taken to a military museum showing its historical equipment and masses of details of their war.

Sadly, I was also taken to a plot of buildings out in the countryside surrounded by woodlands to see yet another mass grave. I was told these poor people were all patients from Vukovar Hospital and the Army were still searching for more graves. One of the buildings had on its inside photographs of those who had been killed. It was obvious by the tiled ground inside these people had also been tortured – no one allowed to walk here, one could only look from the sidelines.

I was also taken to graves of so many young men, each one having a photograph above it.

This was all too much to cope with, it was impossible to stop the tears.

I do not know if I will ever go back to Croatia but this I do know, I shall never forget it.

God Bless them all.

ACKNOWLEDGEMENTS

I dedicate this book to Julie and Adam. I thank them for their love, patience and understanding. I also thank them for never saying, "don't go, Mum". I love you both.

Eventually, it was possible to send over 50 lorries filled with aid of all descriptions to help Croatia.

Perhaps I should mention, through the kindness of people, I received:

Over 50 awards from people in Croatia (Hospitals, Children's Homes, Towns, Churches, and so on)
Bracelet from Duchess of Marborough for Courage and Bravery
Heart of Britain Award 1992
Good Citizen Award 1994
Gloucester Woman of the Year 1997
A medal from the Stroud Rotary which came from America
European Woman of Achievement 1998 (Runner-Up)
A cut glass Decanter from the South West Water Board 1998

None of this was expected but I thank all for their kindness

My thanks also go to Ann and Ken Matthews for without them this book would not be made. Ann kindly offered to type my journals and many pages of writings I had about the war in Croatia. Ken arranged all the photographs, the printing and the shape of how the book would eventually be. I cannot thank them enough for the many hours put into the making of this book along with their constant encouragement and interest. Thank you both so very much.

CONCLUSION

ANOTHER PERSON'S VIEW OF HAZEL HENDRY

This was written in 1999 by someone who nominated me for European Woman of Achievement. I was told 'some people' had nominated me.

Meeting Hazel Hendry is a challenging experience. As is often the case with extraordinary people, she is a very different person to what you might expect. One could be forgiven for imagining a woman who has crossed Europe in a juggernaut, straight into a war zone in order to deliver humanitarian aid, to be a rather formidable character. She is, in reality, a petite, quiet, 50-year something, with a kind open face and a disarming smile. Indeed, she is so apparently 'unremarkable', it is hard to believe this gentle lady has wandered far from Cotswolds, let alone championed 54 highly dangerous missions of mercy to war-stricken Croatians over the course of a decade.

For many, the first natural reaction is 'Why?' Why does a person decide to go where others fear to tread? Why did she feel she could make a difference? Why did she risk her life for strangers? But these are easy questions for Hazel. 'I just felt I was needed', she states simply.

Having already clocked up 15 years of working for *Tear Fund*, Hazel was no stranger to charity work, but her first visit to The Balkans came in 1991. It was in response to a telephone call asking for help from her friend, the Reverend George Hoffman (ex-Chairman of Tear Fund) who was already working in Croatia. Hazel immediately set to work on an appeal. Starting with the local newspapers, giving her project the exposure it needed, she managed to get together several lorry loads of blankets, food, clothes, shoes and medical supplies – in fact anything she could lay her hands on to take to Croatia – and so began her first acquaintance with a people to who she was destined to become inextricably linked.

Although she had initially planned to go out for only two weeks, Hazel hadn't been in the country long, before she found herself profoundly drawn to the Croatians and compelled to help in any way she could. "You need to be among them to understand", she says. "Once I had crouched in street doorways with 90-year old women and young wives with their children, completely terrified as the shells whistled past our ears, I just knew I would be back – there was no hesitation". Although she didn't speak the language, Hazel says there was 'deep communication' between them. "The old women would hold their hearts and then touch mine, or cup my face in their hands and cry".

When George Hoffman was tragically killed in a car crash, Hazel was in no doubt that she had to continue the work. She felt strongly that she 'just had to tell people about the need in a straightforward way' and funds would follow. Her instinct was right for she was to find folk 'very willing to give' – so willing in fact, that with overwhelmingly generous support from schools, churches, companies and individuals, Hazel was able to organise a massive 54 huge assignments in all (one year she managed to send eight). "Each 39-ton lorry cost £2,100 to commission, but the English are inherently generous," she explains, "and funding was never an issue".

Raising the money and collecting the aid, however, was only the beginning. As soon as she had a lorry load, Hazel set her course for Zagreb, located the Front, and made a beeline for it. Each time she went, she discovered a scene far worse that she had anticipated. "I will never forget the suffering etched into the faces of the children and old people", she says, suddenly going quiet. "Hundreds of people fleeing potential massacre, abandoning their villages. Some walking for days – a desperate people.

It didn't take Hazel long to realise that she needed a native driver – "One who knew which roads not to take", she laughs, and more importantly, she had to have an interpreter. The latter she found in a tall, brave Croatian by the name of Darko. "We went through a lot together", she says. "Darko was constantly at my shoulder interpreting and guiding me". Unfortunately, her drivers were sometimes a little less brave and were understandably reticent to drive into red alert areas. 'I'm afraid I once had to resort to stamping my foot and saying, "If *I* can go - why can't you", giggles Hazel. "And amazingly, it worked".

Whilst in Croatia, Hazel would establish from the officials, which other places were in need of aid, before returning home to begin yet another round of fund-raising for such places as Vinkovci, Slavonski Brod, Županja, Čepin and Osijek- and so the work continued throughout the 1991-1996 conflict and beyond. Hazel also made it her business to visit orphanages, hospitals and prisons - simply getting access to a jail, a remarkable achievement in itself. She was the only foreigner to be granted access to the country's jails, thanks to the fact (according to one official) that she was 'a woman doing a man's job!' One important aspect of her work was to measure the limbs of landmine victims so that she could return next time with custom-made prostheses. Often she was a personal target from sniper attack and always, her life was in danger from the shelling. "If you could hear them whistle, then you knew you were still alive", she says soberly.

Asked if she ever despaired, Hazel admits to some secret tears - mixed with anger at times. "When I was sat with patients in a hospital under fire, and there weren't any medical supplies", she says, "or I felt I wasn't doing enough". But inwardly, she believed she was sent for a purpose, and that gave her the strength to continue.

Hazel certainly witnessed her share of horrors and the painful memories will never diminish. "I shall always be haunted by the terrible things I saw", she says sadly. "The mass graves, the awful funerals, my friend, Igor, blown up by a landmine, and 12-year old Slaven, who tried to commit suicide. But there were times of hope too", she smiles, remembering the children tugging at her sleeves to say 'hello', and the sheer joy on the faces of the people when they saw her lorry full of aid roll up.

Hazel's last mission of mercy was in December 1999 when she accompanied a much-welcomed 38-ton lorry absolutely bursting at the seams with aid bound for Pozega, just in time for Christmas. Since then, Hazel has maintained weekly contact with those she befriended in such difficult circumstances.

"The people are still re-building their lives", she reports. In some villages like Lazlovo, quite literally. This is a place which was totally destroyed during the conflict but the villagers have painstakingly rebuilt it piece by piece themselves. With much of the country's industrial infrastructure gone, desperate poverty, and the gruesome legacy of war an ever-present reality, Hazel believes it will be a while yet before things are back to normal. "They tell me they've changed. Things are quieter now, more straightforward. They can go shopping, the hospitals are functioning, some have jobs - but many more don't - they're getting there, but there's still some way to go".

As for Hazel, 44 awards later, a medal from America, and a nomination for 'European Woman of Achievement', she must surely be thinking about putting her feet up. But not Hazel. Having returned to Croatia several times since her last appeal, she never will be able to forget her friends or stop caring passionately about the heart-breaking person burdens left upon them by the finger of tragedy. Awful cases like the aforementioned Igor, his face blown apart by a booby trap whilst he was clearing landmines, now in a vegetative state, cared for by his mother. Or young Slaven, 'kept alive by his parents' love', now sinking away. (He tried to hang himself during an intensive shell attack because he was so terrified).

Such ongoing sorrows mean that despite having being temporarily obliged to 'take a breather' due to ill health, Hazel is once again busy making plans, undertaking speaking engagements, and raising funds and provisions for yet another 'Christmas lorry' of aid to leave this country by the end of October. She is already getting promises of clothes, food, toiletries, and gifts from upcoming Harvest Festival services including a pledge of furniture and linen from a London hotel group, but there is still much to achieve.

Amazingly, after all selfless efforts, Hazel is adamant she is Just an ordinary person - not special'. And yet, clearly, she was and still is, very special indeed to the countless numbers of Croatians who benefitted from her compassion, and who gave her the affectionate title 'Mother of Croatia'.

The Front Line around Osijek, Dakovo, Vinkovci and Vukovar